T0086766

Oh, you thought
this was a date?!

Oh, you thought this was a date?!

Apocalypse Poems   **C. Russell Price**

TRIQUARTERLY BOOKS/NORTHWESTERN UNIVERSITY PRESS
EVANSTON, ILLINOIS

TriQuarterly Books
Northwestern University Press
www.nupress.northwestern.edu

Copyright © 2022 by Northwestern University Press.
Published 2022 by TriQuarterly Books / Northwestern University Press.
All rights reserved.

Interior artwork: Details from Erin Houghtaling, *Untitled*, paper collage (Isolation Series, 2020)

Printed in the United States of America
10 9 8 7 6 5 4 3 2 1

Library of Congress Cataloging-in-Publication Data

Names: Price, C. Russell, author.
Title: Oh, you thought this was a date?! : apocalypse poems / C. Russell Price.
Description: Evanston : TriQuarterly Books/Northwestern University Press, 2022.
Identifiers: LCCN 2022002724 | ISBN 9780810145221 (paperback) | ISBN 9780810145238
    (ebook)
Classification: LCC PS3616.R5247 O35 2022 | DDC 811.6—dc23/eng/20220120
LC record available at https://lccn.loc.gov/2022002724

For Alex Tyk and Melody McCray Eskridge.
I liked this world best when we were together.

Look but don't touch, this skin so sacred
I love my body though I ain't create it
They pay me for it like it's me who made it
Ain't chose this world, I'm just here to take it

—JUNGLEPUSSY

I've never been a boyfriend kind of girl.

—AMY WINEHOUSE

See alone we stand, together we fall apart
Yeah, I think I'll be alright
I'm working so I won't have to try so hard
Tables, they turn sometimes
Oh, someday
No, I ain't wasting no more time

—THE STROKES

Do you see
how I persist in telling you about the flowers when I mean to describe the rain?
—Diane Seuss

If you offered me a passionate love affair and you offered
me a high-priestess role in a fabulous castle above a
cliff where I can just, like, live a very spiritual kind of
religious-library-communing-with-the-stars, learning
kind of existence, I'm going to go for the high priestess.
—Stevie Nicks

Contents

All the Beautiful Men I Touch Myself to Are Dead and Beautiful

I Heard Somebody Say, "Disco Inferno, Burn This Mother Down"

Give Me Two Things: A Lookout & a Shovel

Dance Yourself Clean

Just Because They're Gods, Doesn't Mean You Can't Briefly Disagree

Now Comes in the Fuckery

Off Camera There Is a Beach & a Party

The Devil Has Been Busy Today

You Knew There Had to Be a Reckoning

It's a Nice Day to Start Again, It's a Nice Day for a White Wedding

Pretend a
Pandemic

I don't speak to anyone for a week.
I just sit on a stone by the sea.
—ANNA AKHMATOVA

Apocalypse

1a: One of the Jewish and Christian writings of 200 B.C.E. to 150 C.E. marked by pseudonymity, symbolic imagery, and the expectation of an imminent cosmic cataclysm in which God destroys the ruling powers of evil and raises the righteous to life in a messianic kingdom.

2a: Something viewed as a prophetic revelation

3a: A large, disastrous fire

3b: A great disaster

A relief.

Soundtrack

"So Sad about Us" by The Who

Ritual

In a hot car
with the windows up,
put on a marching band.
I want a stadium inside you.
If you do not have access to a motor vehicle:
in a closet, eat an orange.
You can switch off the sun.

Bud Initiation

Tonight, we take down the scarecrows
and in the fields we light them up.
Against the glow of the orange sky,
we fool ourselves into thinking them real people.
The real trees, the real birds
everything all the time breathing.
I picture my breath into their bodies,
it makes me feel less alone in this plain, this body.
All blue, all black, the sky shines
and we go to bed alone.
I close my eyes, make a wish the world drops
dead, but we still wake up.
I close my eyes as the orange sky
fills with mute ash and real birds.
We flail our arms.
We erect each other into the ether.
This is a kind of love, stuffing each other
with hay, washing our backs with kerosene.

Human Flesh Search Engine

In the taqueria steam, you make me an organ
cooler with your neon-Jack-Daniel's dusty kiss.
The city is in shambles and we're somehow still
breathing within our generation of body stackers.
My sweet, beat me up around the old oak tree;
call me, at least once, your Southern Comfort.
I have measured our love in bottle caps
and beer boxes. I dismantled the ceiling
fan last night because you were so far away
. . . I've been sleepwalking. Happy people kill
themselves all the time to the happy music
we put on as we fuck. My hands: raw, Cloroxed
hummingbirds. The last night you slept
on my green-as-a-sea settee, I soft-shoed
to the kitchen, blew out the pilot,
each shallow breath another knob turning up.
You say: *Ugly girls write the best poetry.*
On my loneliest nights, I slip into someone
else with a bad, blond wig and a coworker's hand
-me-down dress. I dance on every floor
of my apartment building—as if my body is
everything flying out of a wild, unlocked sanctuary—
as if everything unused collapses.

An Anti-Armageddon Poem

If this is
to be my life:

planting flowers
that will die,

writing love poems
to men who'll die—

I'll take it
blossom by blossom by blossom.

There Will Come Soft Rains and the Smell of the Ground

The woods are full of a silence.
I breathe a scrawl of ice in my own darkness
As my gun barks, putting the whole landscape to death.

—Thomas James

Bird

1b: The young of other animals. *Obsolete.*

3: *Sport.* A game bird; with game-preservers *spec.* a partridge. *figurative.* Prey, object of attack.

4a: In various *figurative* applications, chiefly from sense 2; as in reference to the winged or noiseless flight, or soaring of birds; to their confinement in cages; to their song; to the Latin *rara avis* rare fowl, rarity. Also, referring to a (pretended) private or secret source of information.

4c: A prison sentence; prison

4e: An obscene gesture of contempt

In a manic depression, I envisioned myself a hummingbird breeder. An impossibility due to both their protected-species classification and their hostility toward one another when encaged together.

Soundtrack

"Season of the Witch" by Donovan

Ritual

Grow something edible from seed;
at harvest, let it rot.
Write an apology letter.
Dead-eye yourself in a mirror,
whisper the name of everyone
who has wronged you
and who has loved you
and who has done both.
Turn every faucet on.
Burn the letter. Write it again, but better.

Armageddon Origin Story

Someone is
getting molested
in the lake house.

The man next door
is mowing the lawn.
Still the flowers

are blooming. The blotch
growing day by day.
Flood's not the answer,

people just float.

On Reading a Copy of Pushkin I Stole from My Childhood Rapist: A Cento

He daddled me as a small boy,
produced a haze in me. I was
just nine years of age, soul still blossoming out.
I don't know why.
My kith, my kin, three whole hours—
one customary grief each hour, each day.
A roar of violins, violent surging,
just another dumb moon over a dumb horizon.
His thievish mouth all in a blaze
for sport, for the crumbled sofa.
Here there's no conscience; here no sense.
He killed eight years in such a style.
I learned new sadness, unkind terror
and its consolation. How to hiss
him off. Who would have thought it?
I've no one here who comprehends me.
I drink in the midnight.
I walk the shore, I watch the weather,
I see him in dream: pale transcript
of a vivid master. How well he knew
the way to hurt. I only write like this,
you know, because I'm grieving still.
I might have said a word and then thought
day and night and thought again about one thing:
when will the Devil come for you?
I tell my early life, unlock my tongue.
Alright, you want my resurrection:
Thank God, you had no inclination to blow your brains out.

The Poem in Which the Apocalypse Doesn't Go So Terribly

We're in a town ten miles from Tuscaloosa.
We've imported hanging moss because you're sick
of my stories about men
just swinging like that.

Today the news is all good:
because we haven't talked to anyone
and the booze we make in the backyard
is full of only airglow and moonmilk.

Before we moved here, things just fell down:
first a satellite and then, one by one,
planes, birds, and when our house was hit
with a blimp, we felt lucky.

In this town of just the two of us,
I don't question your choke-grip,
you do not hold my wrist for daily inspection.
At night, we fuck the trailer park out of each other.

The men who used to live and burn
things in our mosquito alley would've responded.
As if we were the last coyotes,
as if you could forget why and how a thing howls.

Mr. Doomsday

Your blue jeans are ripped at the crotch
and tonight I'm getting that T-shirt wet.

You make me your handsomest pig as I puff
through your pit patch: your workday armor.

If you are wearing red underwear,
you will want to fuck me while looking at a picture of my sister.

You say with a straight-edge chagrin,
"You can ask only one question. Put on that wig."

I save pleasantries and want only untamable baggage,
I kiss the Needle's party gift,

I lick the Razor's bracelet defeat.
I take you in me to plant a cherry bomb.

Tonight's sex soundtrack is another pretty dead thing.
When the loop begins, it's time to pay up,

shower, get gone. Returning, you smell like me
and I give you one on the house

because I know the sad boy scent.
You pull out with the breaking news.

Anderson Cooper always looks amazing.
The time to unmute the TV and stop jackhammering's arrived.

The latest great flood starts with an unstickable American faucet,
a whole Floridian town with its hands on its hips,

bubble gum smacking: each pop a *So, this is it?*
With you limp beside me, I imagine first the tub, then Tampa,

then the whole South under water. This john will rule
with an iron cock ring and superhero calves.

We will start with the Stars and Bars;
we burn the flag and name the dead.

Your family stops using the N-word,
your parents rainbow bumper sticker the whole state of VA.

This wet earth has no dry land for your bullshit.
The big mouths have been busted and the bullies're buried.

My sex education consisted of touch → kiss → AIDS,
Mr. B., you were wrong and I don't fucking forgive you.

My john and I fuck every day because we're the last left in Chicago.
We pretend the market's still standing and closing at ten.

No other world but this one now.
When my john is gone too long,

I think he's found a third
breathing thing in our fish-tank home.

I wonder if he pays them after, if he says my name
like an abandoned amusement park.

If he simply says, *I'm sorry for bombing*
those islands that you loved.

But about That Day or Hour No One Knows, Not Even the Angels in Heaven, nor the Son, but Only the Father ... Two Men Will Be in the Field; One Will Be Taken and the Other Left

... we are each other's
harvest:
we are each other's
business:
we are each other's
magnitude and bond.
—Gwendolyn Brooks

Kingdom

1: A politically organized community or major territorial unit having a monarchical form of government headed by a king or queen

2: Often capitalized

2a: The eternal kingship of God

2b: The realm in which God's will is fulfilled

4b: The spiritual realm of evil or infernal powers; the rule of such powers

Younger and tasked with the imaginary act of sacrificing a family member or a boy I was in love with, I chose myself for the betterment of everyone.

Soundtrack

"I'm On My Way" by Barbara Dane

Ritual

If you have survived up until now unwounded; you
are a tragic miracle and I don't trust you.
Go a day without food and pick a new vice to test-
drive instead.
For your first recovery meal, is there gravy? Did you
even suffer a little this day with a useless mouth?

Our Love Transcends Sexuality & Gender & Time & Place; Translation: Not Now, Not Ever

This world is not right
for us, so I sit
you down and work
a new one, all hollers
and honeysuckle, all blue
and gloriously crushing.

In this assessment of intention,
you finally carry my body
and my cape of little rejections
back to ol' Virginia
and make me up like
I would have wanted.

How tired are you now
when you reach the cherry-lined street?
Do the lilacs say *thank you*?
No—not there—not beside the collie kennel
that only once howled louder than me.
There: at the foot of the drive:

cross me, cat-eye me with ash,
call me by my dead name one last time.
Kiss my cheek and think cul-de-sac,
think normative fence, think, my love,
of all the stars where better versions are breathing,
where the soft-focused-wanted me slowly wakes.

Someone Is Missing for You and the Whole World Feels Empty

We're on LSD going eighty in a downpour.
The emergency Xanax I keep in a necklace begs.

There was some aching in me
that I knew was aching in you.

Coyote, I am terrified of the grief
you've reached before me like a track mark.

Once in my early, wild haze for you I casually asked
for your favorite song like a latchkey.

The seventeen-minute file was meant a comical challenge,
a song your mother played to outcool your friends.

Coyote, the casserole would be too chilled
by the time it reached you by CTA.

I was such a messy, big secret.
I don't want to bring whispers to her funeral.

Beside you, the woman you chose is comforting
in a way that I am unable or unwanted to do.

Coyote, here is a fun fact about flowers: they're just flowers.
I am fighting the Leo in me trying to make your loss mine.

The closest you let me get to meeting your mother
was her folding an Old Navy shirt you borrowed.

I am working out how to lift what now hangs
around you, give me your sadness in fistfuls and boatloads.

At night, always at night, you will want a howl
to drown it all out, a thrash, a mosh escape.

Coyote, come over when you want. I am always
awake with my own brand of American sadness.

I am turning down the rain for you.
I am salting the sidewalk with wildflowers.

If You Want Space, Join NASA

When I am
in my sickness
no one wants
to stay around.

What of me
will you put
in your shadow
box, blue memorial?

I say to you
what I want
someone to say
to me: *I'm not leaving*

my apartment today
for anything but
to sing
into your mouth.

For a little bit
of my little life,
we are
such lovely little things.

I feel so shameful
falling in love
while there are children
in cages.

Tell me the way
you want to neck
and make love
at the end of the world

before the night comes
when they come
to take my lovers.
They will come.

I am simple:
I want to fuck 'em
up, jaw break,
and loogie slug.

I raise my arms
and a wave of vengeance
grows with my improbability
to have survived so long.

Again, what was done
to me will not undo me.
There's no sin

in becoming kind
to our bodies.
I rooted for you
and you appeared

to live a life
we've made in song.

We Fold the Flag and Name the Dead

The bootlegger and the postmaster,
a pajama gambler with a Nashville sister,
blue tattered men sexing in a Methodist parking lot,
the healers and their dried-up springs,
the smoking hairdresser with Milli Vanilli
posters, the tree blooming a Jeep like a busted bud,
the suicide, the suicide, the next ones,
decades of corsages and funeral arrangements,
a man who collects cans along the highway,
the boys who threw rocks, the boys, the boys, the boys

Hush Money

It became an outright lie
and even though I dressed the body
it was still naked, still killed.
It was caught
in the first place at birth,
like a fish.
But I played it, dressed it up,
dressed it up like somebody's doll.

—ANNE SEXTON

Poverty

1a: The state of one who lacks a usual or socially acceptable amount of money or material possessions

1b: Renunciation as a member of a religious order of the right of an individual to own property

2: Scarcity, dearth

3a: Debility due to malnutrition

3b: Lack of fertility

When confronted with his crimes and their continued effects, my childhood molester got me a Blue Apron trial subscription and paid my rent for a few months.

Soundtrack

"Dead of Night" by Orville Peck

Ritual

Outside your front door, scatter a spice
or herb you do not know
the colonizing history behind.
Count all the triangles you see
around you, remember how .
triangles consume people: molasses
to rum to slaves.
Write down the name of every family member
you have (without any help).
Write their sins.
Write down yours.
Tape these pages from your front door
to the front door of the closest financial institution.
What? Were you expecting a church?
Rule #1: Do not bite the hand that feeds you.
　　　Rule #2: Do not get caught doing it.

On When They Say Hustling, They Don't Mean Dicking Down a Stranger

It is impossible to walk away from a man with a car and cocaine. This escort loves loves loves your library. I ask you if you are going to murder me. You laugh. I laugh. I always think the john might murder me. Cruising always feels on the edge of Armageddon. Have you ever considered how much emotion is buried in a 7-Eleven parking lot? Maybe it's my sickness talking again? I know my BPD is in control when I could fuck the wall if it called me pretty. When the wallet says *take me* as he's pushing my head down, I hear seven trumpets in the bass beat blasting through my portable speaker. I won't make love without music; I have to keep count. An hour is only an hour. I've made a commodity of my coping mechanisms. How strange I haven't swallowed myself for what was done to me that I can't undo. I am simple in the Anthropocene. I wanna fight and I wanna fuck and I've gotta make money. I like the people the most that I don't have to love all the time. My greedy therapist must love what a treasure chest I am. I make everyone cum like honey in a Texas drought. All your neighbors can tell by your yell that I spell my name with double S and double L. If you want me to cry in the middle of it, say so, my depression is a stubborn Pisces and I am your Hunger God and I make you feel special. Work is work is work is work. Remind me my name I'm calling myself tonight. Tonight, no one's getting murdered.

I Did an Ugly Thing Once, but It Was in a Beautiful Room

When I knelt
at the Temple of Nature,
I keened, *O! Wreck me,*
wreck my guts, Daddy.

I have given everything
to the earth that has pulled me
through a lonely winter.
What if I had loved you only enough?

We emptied the dishwasher, we ritualized
to incite self-induced preservation.
Don't you ache not to die?
Baby, I feel so down—turn me on.

Through the tall grass: a slither,
a woman taken by the wind,
the Pepsi-Cola sign, the seagulls, the noise.
In my grief over you, I run off

with a grad of the school of dope tattoos.
I give myself to a man with a dark plume.
He imagines a world without art: it's not bad.
Poetry is often just another form of content.

You were my absolute favorite vapor flower
in the garden of the world. There's such
a thing as suffering. I pray to the moon,
I touch myself and you are alive again.

The Tsunami Was Not a Metaphor. For a Full Day I Was the Drowning Wave

You're perfect at making me believe
cyanide is wine, my playmate,
my little curb-stomped Coke can.
Our dog is dead. Your phone is dead.
I hijack a plane to skywrite your name.
I could go back to the city
or another, or just wander around the lake.
I could stand all day shouting *Leon Leon Leon*
into the Grand Canyon's blistered mouth.
I don't. I put one leg after the other
and stack the world on my chest at night.
I find a man and then a few more—
imagine their shoulder blades yours—
I squint as I hydroseed their happy trail.
After the binge—that one, not the others—
I woke up beside you with the terrible
sin of contempt. You said *soulmate* like a goddamn jingle,
like a suicide ultimatum.
As you slept beside me, I twisted my hair
like a hanging tree. I rubbed the small
of your back like the rim of a hotdish
small-town secret. When I kissed you good-bye
in front of the neighbor's Chihuahua,
the sidewalk, the gangbangers,
I meant: *This world has been enough already,*
if only for this wanting:
the apartment always on the edge
of going up into glorious strip-teased flames.

How to Die on a Farm

The vegetarians have slipped
and cannibalism is on its way.

Just go ahead without me,
put on Fleetwood Mac:

I am a simple Stevie spinning,
you motherfucker.

What keeps me here:
a cat, cheap beer,

hair dye, good weed,
a beautiful man laughing

from a distance, this picture
of Earth—everything

that has ever been.
A blue ball spinning.

Pack your fanny pack
and don't look back.

Let's flip those 11 A.M. tables
at Applebee's. Let's make it out

of this alive, let's toss
salads and give head.

Quietly backstage, I've scribbled
destructive fuck dreams.

Outside, miraculously, the world
continues and the pile of red flags

in a man-suit says *I'm so bad*
I should have brought knee pads.

I've emptied the world
of men like him.

I want the ash
of your tongue

in the little cherry
of my tough palm.

There's no such thing
as an OK age

to go missing,
to be missed.

You will know me,
how important I am,

by the blue petals
I leave in my wake.

Double Fisting at a Gay Sex Club Because a Man Is Buying Me Drinks So He Can Watch Me Pee and I'm Thinking of You

I am not slowed.
I brought that protection
and I know my power.
I've found a beautiful song
I cannot show you now.
I came in here,
the only girl in the world,
wearing nothing
but my sad like a harness.
A mirrorball, a spitshine,
a flashglare—he licks
my retreat. Someone left
the back door unlocked; someone let
themselves inside. The men I love
are balding like volcanoes,
collapses of coarseness and color.
In my heart I built
a scrap-paper mill to you.
I am lonely even here,
full of self-confidence and pills.
We open our chainsaw mouths;
we go back home
to touch ourselves alone.
You used to ask about my day.

All the Beautiful Men I Touch Myself to Are Dead and Beautiful

The lovesick, the betrayed,
and the jealous all smell alike.
—COLETTE

Promenade

1: A leisurely walk, *esp.* one taken in a public place so as to meet or be seen by others. Also (occasionally): a ride or drive taken in this manner.

2c: British. An area without seats at a theater or concert venue; *spec.* a gallery at a music hall, commonly thought to be frequented by prostitutes and their clients (now historical)

3a: In country dancing: a movement resembling a march made by couples in formation

A sad prom is still a prom.

Soundtrack

"Fancy" by Bobbie Gentry

Ritual

Get drunk in front of your cat,
practice an important speech,
like a breakup or resignation.
The next morning tell
your boss and that dude
they aren't shit via group text.
Say your cat got ahold of your phone,
but the message holds true.
Ruin your life a little, then ruin a lot.

Sweetwater, Texas

1

It's not that I'm not listening to you,
it's just the same day but a different year.

It's that in this moment, one year ago, the only girl
I ever grapevined with was shot in the face.

Rebecca, I needed you to hate myself
less. I had to pretend

as long as possible as our streets
became paved with memorial stones.

2

Before prom, before organza girls were to be pricked
by corn-fed boys' corsages, Aaron sat in his Jeep.

Seven A.M. was a strange time to leave
and sit among his horses, cleaning an unshot gun.

The bang came between the bacon sizzle and the omelet flip.
His mother must have known, with her white streak, what

she'd hold in her white apron as the chickens coo'ed.
Aaron, I've never told anyone of our buckle to buckle,

your pause and breath, the look of you saying:
Please, please, don't tell a fucking soul.

3

Ms. Spence's hands shook like Mr. Skipper's
when he cut the cord hanging his daughter,

Nikki, from the tree. Whatever she was thinking
seventh period is unclear. How she could have been

swinging so long unseen is unforgivable. Her arms
were *too* burly, her skin *too* dark.

After kickoff, the stadium buzzed
with her front yard ElectraCord self-lynching.

All the other Nikkis looked, out and over the pigskin
and leafbreeze, the goalposts, to the Methodist

cemetery where a hundred teenagers looked down
into the darkest of new ditches.

4

Last April, the first tornado came through
in my town's history. The gas pumps spraying,

the Wendy's completely rubbled, and a river
of crushed caskets met the dividing creek

knocking into cars like Clydesdales,
an orchestra of alarms, one final parade

to bring back seventh grade, our hips sweating
in another's palms. Aaron and Nikki:

you come back when it's sunny and I'm in love,
when I kiss someone,

I see you in their yellowjacket lashes.
If I had been out,

would the lunchroom have been bearable?
If I had been braver, would you be

in my driveway, waiting with a warmed car,
ready to drive away as fast as we can?

5

Every day, I walk with a private loneliness,
like being a golden mutt-mix let out

on an abandoned Tennessean farm, discovering
for the first time, it'll never see

a single truck again.

Desiree Says, "There Were Crisis Actors at the Crucifixion of Jesus Christ"

I'm poolside in Tampa
with my new stripper friends
from the Déjà Vu Danceteria.

I'm talking about doomsday again
and we're taking turns on the blunt
while listing our favorite scenarios.

You can always tell a lot about someone
by how they roll and how they want the end
to happen. Fire and ice are so passé.

Maybe nothing says more about American boredom
than by how well-fleshed we imagine Armageddon.
The dancers and I are splashing now,

shouting lavish demises: angels of punishment,
islands of cannibal horses, a vacant Kmart
parking lot. We're always elsewhere

when the shit goes down: in the romance
of airport hotels, the sluggish arms of local barflies,
beneath a big black sky opening in your hometown.

Then, Brother, Get Back, 'Cause My Breast's Gonna Bust Open

If there's no water,
you can't drown.
If there's no elsewhere,
there's nowhere
to go missing.
Brother river-kissed
brother ash-scattered.
I shadow my eyes
every morning in a simple weep.
You called me a cool stupid fuck.
You loved me
you loved me
you loved me
like something easy.
Your goneness never stops.
I slip into the harness,
I deathgrip an invisible safety,
I stare down into the corkscrew:
I swallow the whole spiral.
We were never about butterflies.
I say: *you are even here in my fear.*
I itch; you scratch back.

My Sweetheart Is a Drunkard, Lord, He Drinks down in New Orleans

You should have settled for a honey jar
in a vein of the hill where harebells broke & faded.
I must have been unwieldy as a python bobbing
on a surface of white flowers—you pulled away
from me & went on
as bullfrogs tuned their bassoons for autumn.

Before I brought you to this strange autopsy,
we lived, alone, in a town where everyone died of hunger.
Eating the heart out of this room,
I ride your sea-garden of lost letters.
Tonight, I go out searching for you everywhere
as the passionflowers whisper of you over & over.

I Heard Somebody Say, "Disco Inferno, Burn This Mother Down"

They reel me in, a displaced anchor.
The cygnets scatter. I rise, I nod,
Wrapped in a jacket of dark weed.
I dangle, I am growing pure,
I fester on this wooden prong.
An angry nail is in my tongue.

—Thomas James

Reckoning

1a: The action or an act of accounting to God after death for (one's) conduct in life; an account so given; the occasion of giving such an account, the Last Judgment. Also: God's judgment on or penalty for a person's actions.

1b: The action or an act of giving or being required to give an account of something, *esp.* one's conduct or actions; an account or statement so given. Also: an occasion of giving or being required to give such a statement; a calling to account.

1c: A momentous occasion or period; a turning point

After an intervention, I discover repressed memories and an inhuman amount of rage.

Soundtrack

"It's Too Late" by Carole King

Ritual

With an adult's supervision,
burn something, anything small and unmissable in your alleyway or cul-de-sac.
Slowly add small things of sentimental value to the burn pile:
ticket stubs from beige dates with balding men, tissue paper or wrapping from
    a dead friend's gift,
a Post-it mantra that kept you out of the hospital and unsuicided.
If you do not have a small phrase keeping you alive (still?!),
use the space below:

Tend to the fire until things get out of control and you have nothing left.

Oh Baby, I Hope When They Take You They Take Me Too

All men have been castrated for health
and public safety. Sorry.
We reached a point of postmodernism,
it hinged on negligence.
A crisis is a crisis
until resolution. Hence: castration.
The clinics are clean, free, and close by.
Emotional violence has a twin
in the physical form.
We don't use metaphors for rape
or war anymore
because there aren't rapes
or wars anymore.
Everyone has so many rights
now more than before.
There's less overtalk
in the last generation of fathers.
If we are to live in ruins,
we might as well enjoy it.
The cicadas are red hot
in this glorious new world
where cargo shorts're still allowed.
A pocket is a beautiful, necessary thing.

I Think We're Alone Now: Your Lips, My Lips, Apocalypse

they throw him like a cigarette butt
three stories shoeless blindfolded at the base
children hold stones in case the fall doesn't
do the trick the crowds cheer as he's flipped
over the ledge across the world hate pulls up
in a pick-up truck opens his door says *pretty boy*
why are you walking alone get in I know
what loneliness tastes like he thinks
as his thighs stick to the interior
they call it the little death and we always
end up looking up at a world shaking us out the sky
an unbearable blue grass so green
everything has to hurt

Death Comes for the Good Ol' Boys

in a gown of royal blue.

She lines them up with relentless discretion,
she lines them up by their pretty smiles.

She says to her women: *Unhinge your jaws, bite
the hand, then devour the heart.*

The year of the new cannibal Amazon started with Brenda
(from accounting) who, when over-pinched,
started chomping on her boss's knuckles.

Ten years later Sox stadium is the new Colosseum.
The women place bets and eat fried men-thighs.
The fighters fight because men are good
for only two things in this world: breeding and eating.

Here—everyone's a little gay by necessity.

Kesha rules all and the man-cages reek
of what men do to one another.

Not even the last computer can recite the sound
of a male perceived pronoun.

In this apocalypse, we raise our boys until we can break them,
then bone-feed our front yards.

Why Can't My Heaven Be a Mobile Home Park in a Carolina Where I Have Big Hair and Work Reception at My Husband's Tattoo Parlor?

I've been reading a lot about Canadian men
and chemical castration. When my lover pulls out
my depression: he says *Russell, I'm certain the panic is over.*
He knows the river asks me for a breezeblock kiss,
how the sad-eyed dragonflies in my body want
a tornado spotting—oh, there,
there, there he is again waiting for me across the bar.
If he loved me, he'd release an EP.
He calls me a mixture of beauty-
queen hair and trailer-park attitude.
I leave my keys in the door. I would if I could turn
the corner and end up in Spain. On the good days,
he wants me on my baddest behavior.
He picks my polish and then I blow
each digit as if it's a double barrel.
The older I get, the more ghosts I gather.
It's 2022 and I need some simple happiness
like a sundress with cavernous pockets
and a fresh switchblade.
My great gender trouble as a queer American
is that I should think "erect"
not "automatic rifle" when I hear "semi."
He asks about the men in my past, the archive of grief:
the first-boyfriend-who-loved-you-but-not-in-public,
the next who thinks of me then quickly stops himself,
the one who marries late in life and if you squint you're the bride,
the man who, I told my mother, touched me in the paper aisle of the Piggly.
I tell him I have only learned that you can forgive,
but you can't stick around—that we won't get out of county
because we're bad and free.
When I call him after a proper cry in the office supply closet,
he asks what is drowning me today, as if memory is a growing leak,

as if he could offer some Oprah-level shit.
Without a doubt, I say
that in my family there was a Klansman.
That in that house, a white man killed
a BIPOC because of: terror, war, circumstance, 'cause
they could get away with it
and stay silent because I didn't ask.
Something is eating me belt, watch, and all,
I say to him, *sweetheart, this claptrack's been waiting for you.*

Give Me Two Things: A Lookout & a Shovel

We make our own masks: sand dollars
tied behind the head with kite string. . . .
I live in the richest country in history, or so I hear.
There are no green zones, only shrapnel
we cannot feel or see.
We go to work with the bodies we have.

—Amit Majmudar

Rent

1d: The produce of a crop, fruit

2d: *(a)* Money, cash, *esp.* that acquired by criminal activity or in exchange for homosexual favors; *(b)* (hence in extended use) a rent boy; rent boys collectively

According to law, the state in which the crime is committed holds jurisdiction. When we both moved away I mouthed "extradition" every night until I lost my senses. I never went back for a decade. When you went home last Christmas, I itched to call someone for once. We all went to school with the county deputies. We know everyone by name.

Soundtrack

"Tears Dry on Their Own" by Amy Winehouse

Ritual

If there are alleys where you are,
follow one to a farmers' market.
It's your favorite season; tell yourself
that as you strum the strawberries.
As toxic as it sounds, someone loves you
and how you chew.
Do your hair like a beauty queen, try not to
get too drunk getting ready.
What would be so unbearable about being
loved without conditions?
You have just enough time
to paint your eyes as the pie bakes.
Put your old accent back on.
Lend him some sugar.
Whatever comes after the bubbling runoff,
take the nice Jewish boy to the lake;
the next morning at sunrise
whisper to the water all the nice things
you say to each other.
"Anything goes." And you mean it.

Armageddon via Telephone Wires

I'm seventeen and I call my molester
from the last NYC pay phone.
When that last breathy hello echoes,
I slam the receiver against the coin slot
and we laugh and we laugh,
the phone booth and me.
In that untraceable call,
I call you out and I take the sun
back to the sky.
I fall back in love with holidays
and rooms in a family home
ruined by genuflecting and *you like this, faggot,*
don't you?
The man I almost killed myself over
said (when I told him about you):
You're too much, I can't do this, I can't do you anymore
and I stopped talking all together.
During the mute cutting years,
I ate the hole away with fast food
and binges and private purges.
Now when a man introduces himself
with your demon name, I recast him
as something primitive:
I call him a beast.
I call him buttercup.
I have slept with four men
who share your Christian moniker
and each time they bled
I pictured you out of my life all together.
I dream a world of no more B___s.

After Growing Bored with Synonyms for the Apocalypse, I Rename It Carl (a Man with Intricate Tattoos, a Large Penis, and a Coup de Ville)

Carl misses the interruption of commercials.

Carl didn't know about the cover, forgot cash, but swears he'll get you next time.

Carl uses the words "kitsch" and "quirky" too often and incorrectly.

Carl kisses with his eyes open and his hands begging for something he feels entitled to.

Carl's a shitty tipper and a reckless driver; he prescribes positive self-talk.

Carl deadnames without hesitation or worry of recourse.

Carl, lately, has a lot of thoughts on abortion.

Carl is a troubled man who doesn't do therapy because he doesn't believe in it.

Carl likes chairs backless and gender binary.

Carl awaits a tropical storm named just after him.

Carl says there's a racist in his family, but doesn't tell you that it's him.

Carl is NO fats and NO femmes.

2022 Carl still calls things "so gay."

After gay sex, Carl says, "Did you hear that?" Even though you both know there wasn't a sound. He just likes to look at you all up in a panic at the unknown.

Carl mumbles so you have to say "what?" so he can hear himself twice.

Carl is definitely married and works in visual merchandising, but doesn't say where exactly because he isn't out and you have the reputation for just showing the fuck up.

Carl wants us to give veganism a "go" and uses the word "team" too much.

Carl says, "It has recently come to my attention," as if a fact did not exist due to his unknowing of it.

Carl is above all else a troubled man undeserving of my attention, but the sex is good even though he wears hoodies in the middle of August.

Carl never reciprocates oral sex and admits he might have some issues and looks to you for confirmation. Oh, Carl.

Carl says he is superstitious of black cats, but really it's because he's racist and still uses the word "urban."

Carl loves licorice.

Carl believes in trans rights, but has a genital preference.

Carl sings along real loud to the hard-R parts.

Carl loves sleet.

Carl and cancel culture are in heat.

Carl hands you a dirty washcloth from under the bed.

Carl is always almost there or on his way in perpetuity.

Carl is man over party except in the voting booth.

Carl has infringed rights and a repulsion toward collective accountability.

Carl loves a hem undoing itself.

Carl breaks things in his garage with the door open.

Carl doesn't do social media, but has accounts to keep tabs.

Carl, at his absolute best, is 2 P.M. on a Tuesday in February.

Carl can and will get a gun.

Carl is body positive except for scarred fat bodies.

Carl says "secret" too easily, like he has a lot of them.

Carl said "I'm sorry" once and once only and it was on a bleak winter day when he was eleven and said he'd never say it again because a woman made him.

Carl is one bad day away from becoming the harbinger of breaking news.

Carl goes on long drives.

Carl goes on long drives at night behind a bug-graveyard windshield and sunglasses, Hall & Oates, a few cracked beers, windows down.

Carl drives slower the shorter the skirt.

Carl just needs a minute of your time, sweetie.

Carl's a gentleman after all; he opens the child-safe door for you.

Carl gets too close—then closer—his beard wax glimmering—you know not to.

Carl licks his stache roof.

Carl looks at you looking at him as he locks the doors.

Dance Yourself Clean

How they reached the vanishing point I do not remember.
There is no way to get back
through this long succession of addicts

whose guilt is my inheritance,
you have noticed I am heir to the old decisions.
No one contests the sum of such a legacy.

—Thomas James

Surrender

1a: To yield to the power, control, or possession of another upon compulsion or demand

2a: To give (oneself) up into the power of another, especially as a prisoner

2b: To give (oneself) over to something (such as an influence)

3c: The delivery of a fugitive from justice by one government to another

4: An act of rendering (thanks). *Obsolete.*

I have an hour-long recording of you confessing and sobbing, not because you're sorry, but because you got caught. You said it and you wrote it out. You did it. I set my ringtone to your begging.

Soundtrack

"Bad Girl" by Lee Moses

Ritual

Litter a lot
you do not own
with surface-loving seeds.
Pass it everyday
until someone you don't know
mows all the almosts down.
You could have had a yard
full of wildflowers,
and instead—instead, this?

How to Stay Politically Active While Fucking the Existential Dread Away

> Bang your tambourine! kiss
> my ass, don't mind if they
>
> say it's vicious—they don't
> know what music should do to you.
>
> —FRANK O'HARA

It's November and the dead
should stay dead.
There is no script for this,
this life, your lemon seeds
on my kitchen island.
The woods are full
of people like you,
all positive self-talk
in a lynching country.
I think I'll miss you forever.
Once in a Freudian-driven love,
I lived near a water tower
with a snack basket
and he called me his favorite
pampered little suburb bitch.
I center myself on his gun
control and pour some salt
as if we were never here.
I am queering this shit from the inside.
No matter how many shapes I change:
I am an animal.
Forgive me of my humble dreaming
I'll do whatever it is
that you want me to do
to you. Stop, right now. Burn
some sage and play "Runaround Sue."

Come back when you've reached the chorus.
Come see me
on Tuesdays and Thursdays—
what have you got to lose?
I miss your ankles so much,
I taste it in my throat.
Ever since, I have felt like a beautiful stranger
at a nonprofit-sponsored cocktail party.
There are addictions to feed
and mouths to pay. Trash
is trash is trash is trash.
On a Thursday, after a salad,
you ate me out and threw my love up.
I forgive you. I forgive myself. I release the situation.
I am blue, and unwell, you make me bolt
like a horse that stands around
my bedroom making things cry.
I like to drink and take pictures;
I want everyone to have good sex.
But don't you forget about the dark woods.
Can't you hear me
calling, begging you to come out and play.
Enter a synth and call my mountain ranges
by their proper names. I'm doing this
for my younger, suicidal queer self.
Pity isn't a usable currency. I don't care
how you feel about vengeance as justice
in five words or less.
All day, I've thought of reentering The Closet
for safety's sake. A commissioned buzz cut,
muted earth clothes, all baritone.
My God, my God, my mother
still asks about you.
Promise, when you're done with me,
you'll burn everything I ever loved.

When Someone Asks My Gender I Say a Nonexistent Month

I want so much
to say so much.

All my life I've seemed to be
just a funny little thing.

I look in the mirror and try to love
my body, my existence, my death rate

which have recently become subject
to academic discourse and projection

while a cis man signs
another bill to kill me.

I've made terrariums of hurt
out of men in my fishnets.

I broke a jaw in houndstooth
as I told the can't-hear-NO-man

I'm going to be a lady one day;
I don't know when or how.

I adjust the tuck;
I crack my knuckles.

I'm an all-out;
I'm a good-time seed.

Ars Poetica: We Can Take Our Turn, Singing Them Dirty Rap Songs

The world needs more drag
-you-out-into-the-street poetry—
enough with the dishwashing
watching your kid throw a fuck
-ing baseball for the first time.
Give me all that you can't pick up
the phone and tell someone.
No more *souls*
or *truth* or *freedom*—abort
your breathy abstractions.
All my (wo)men moderately pissed off,
come to the page ink-tongue spitting.
The best of all the dirty words is:
complacency—next to: normative—next to:
meta. And for the writer who's breathing
without seething over love's legality
or the sensitivity of someone else's womb—
I've got something for his punk ass:
trigger after trigger of untouchable topics,
a love for the words *pussy* and *chartreuse*,
a whole catalog of men (ass shaking) lines.
Boy, where you came from
is not where you are. E. Bishop,
the baddest of all bitches, said *write it,*
Yoshimi, it'd be tragic if those evil robots
win. If we settled for so much mediocre meditation
(the fluff, fluff, pass of cute poems),
I'd order a recession
on all your bullshit.
Some books should be burned.
Can you hear the gear-flick of my Bic
hungry for all those darlings you've wasted?

My Sexual Identity Is a Toaster in a Bathtub

In the last heather field,
I keep sane with pop sugar:
I'm the kind of guy who laughs at a funeral—
can't understand what I mean, you soon will.
I have the tendency to wear my mind on my sleeves,
I have a history of taking off my shirt
and I say and I sing
lines I never loved
the first go-around, but everything's sore,
I've made myself a siren too often.
If somebody heard me and loved me:
they would have told me by now.
Love, I'm squalling about your nose
tomorrow when I reach what's left
of Texarkana. It's been 888 nights
since I finally left the house
we could never afford. Your dead body *is*
seven cities away and that house:
all Mr. Blue Sky shingle-crowned burned down.
How? Let's say—why save something
that never felt your footsteps?
I'm living in this constant museum,
this world of Why-I-Miss-You's,
my beard a half halo of lavender,
an everyday red-faced soundscape
of what's left and what *else* is left.
If something like you still walked upright,
he'd find me on this last single patch of parakeet green,
and, shaking me, he would stop
the sleep-singing, the coo of *I've got so much honey,*
the bees envy me.

Just Because They're Gods, Doesn't Mean You Can't Briefly Disagree

I am full of the old fear of coming home,
stopping in darkness under the maples.

—Thomas James

Glade Spring, Virginia

A town in Washington County, Virginia, with a population of 1,374 at the 2000 Census, 402 families. The age range at the time: 22.9% under the age of 18, 7.1% from 18 to 24, 26.3% from 25 to 44, 25.5% from 45 to 64, and 18.2% who were 65 years of age or older. For every 100 females, there were 85.7 males. For every 100 females age 18 and over, there were 85.0 males. The town has an area of 1.3 sq miles, all of it land. Established in 1778, the name derives from the Native American word "Passawatami," meaning "This Is the Place."

This is the wound.

Soundtrack

"Up the Wolves" by the Mountain Goats

Ritual

With the assistance of the US Postal System and the trust of someone you know or someone desperate enough for quick cash, have yourself mailed a pound of earth from your hometown. Preferably, the front yard of a pivotal house. Sleep with the soil stowed away in a useless pillowcase for a week. Fuck with it beneath your bottom.

Virginia, 1999, Approaching Y2K

The snapdragons are Methodists singing
sweet tea for everyone—even for the chalk nubs
that once made the fault-cracked driveway an ocean.

Everything is wild: the honey
-suckle, the berries, the animals
caught in cages at night: immovable lightning bugs.

John Lennon crawls out the window
as my mother does casserole dishes.
Back in the yard, my father's digging

a grave or a garden. Before a stranger
stole the kickball sun midair, everything
smelled fresh blue-paint coated, that new black-tar scent.

Alone in a tree someone would soon swing
from, I made myself a million others:
not tobacco-farm married, not even one streetlight.

Inside a withering forsythia bush, I am a witch
doctor with my neighbor's compost
peppers. I'm carving your name into dirt.

I'm learning backroads, blue highways, the whole zoo
sky to show you one Sunday—a few decades from now—
where we forget the city and then the sales tax,

the city before that, and the gearshift, and then:
(as if) the body (only left with right turns)
opens up to an unending forest.

Trying to Catch a Deluge in a Paper Cup

There was something in the water
that gave the guns their names.
You can't feel love
or hate toward something you can't name.

Around us, around the Costco,
around the dog tied up,
we adore our little war zone.
The American economy is thriving
on sympathy cards and bullets in bulk.

Maybe you force yourself to forget
a lot of high schools that've been shot up,
maybe you swallow and forget the temples,
the banks, the libraries, the sidewalks,
the factories, the hospitals, the festivals,
the funerals that've been littered with brass casings.
There are more mass shootings than days in a year.

My parents are chaperoning a prom again;
the art teacher has a handgun in her handbag.
How is this a life we've made?
Even the robins are losing
their goddamn minds.

It Passed for Feathers

Mother, when faraway,
leaving this world,
forgive the awkwardness,
the despair you were
unable to conceal,
the want to hear
an atom bomb record.
Witness—the devil finch—
the still marsh—machine tragedy—
an opera with a lonesome
heroine underwhelming
like sea glass.
It was dark long before
the discovery of elements.
Draw me.
Draw me.
Draw me
after you
with a diamond in my mouth.

The Glove

On fields of brick dust,
beside the trailer park,
he winds up and he winds up
knocking me down
to my knees with a skeetering
groundball. Popcorn has started
birdchirping and the concession-stand lady's
pepperoni hair mats to her pimpled head.
He lifts his leg like a slow-mo hurdle,
his elbow juts out like a warship cannon—
he is throwing everything
at me: the Cleveland suburb,
the how I met your mother night,
all the minor league meals
living off library coupons in Ogden.
I have saved his cellophaned collection of cards
and the rubberband-bound glove.
When, if, he calls, I can tell
the extra gray around his mouth
sings through the hip pain,
the hereditary hypochondria.
When his father died in June,
I sank myself on a Chicago platform.
I raised my lonely leg and my sad little arm,
I swung until the world spun again.

Now Comes in the Fuckery

I want to be important. By being different.
And these girls are all the same.

—Sylvia Plath

Consent

1a: Voluntary agreement to or acquiescence in what another proposes or desires; compliance, concurrence, permission

4a: Agreement in feeling, sympathy; also, more generally, harmony, accord, agreement

A child cannot consent. But a grown person can destroy you.

Soundtrack

"Your Woman" by White Town

Ritual

Drink a tallboy of Mountain Dew or
    your pop of choice. Drink another.
In the hollow cans, empty yourself.
White knuckled and caffeine crazed,
    take yourself and your canteens of
    piss to the site of an early trauma.
    You should be smart enough to
    know what to do next.
Eat berries and think of all of this as
    some sort of healing rather than a
    misdemeanor.
Or do nothing and stay stewing where
    you're at and how you are.

And How Can It Be That This Means Nothing to Anyone but Me Now

In the Chicago Methodist church basement,
the Eating Disorder Recovery group meets
on Tuesdays. We talk about metaphors
for depression, bulldozers we want to bury us.
We take a second of silence for Jenny,
the yo-yo self-proclaimed queen
of pity-fuck kingdom.
Someone says the middle of the universe tastes
like raspberries and that to sloths
hibiscus flowers taste like chocolate.
I'm telling you this because I have something
to say that I keep talking about in church basements.
When I was nine, when the touching started, I spent
days tracing an anatomical heart
over and over and over and over.
My life has been nothing
more than an invisible list of defeats.
Everyone acts so surprised I haven't killed
myself already and that's a lot to live up to.
According to longitudinal studies and the Sister
of Holy Sadness and Purging next to me in recovery,
there's so much intersectionality between sexual assault
and self-harm and I, total shithead, smirk at the idea
of me and the 'rexies built for the apocalypse.
Fate will not stop me from trying
for a sunny day, a cow-tipping expedition,
boys showing up with a keg of beer in a pickup truck.
Nothing is weird about nightstand Nutella.
No strangeness in blacking out an entire decade.
Once, a man buried a purple carnation bulb
in my left breast and the *why* was nowhere,
not even in the Chincoteagues.

When your house caught fire, I wanted you
in it. I dream about finding you
in the parking lots of Hell. You, me, and too many men
who've never heard the good word *no*
and understood it and stopped.

A Household God

When the bomb hit the poor town
next to us, we were on our lunch break
having loud and holy afternoon sex.

When we hear the news, we go
at it again like feral hogs.
We need this to get through all the rest.

I don't want to die but I don't care
if I die now praying for you
to go harder, to make a scupper of me.

What stupid luck we have to have
survived up till now, all this
evolution and this is how we want to waste it.

A Love Poem Will Not Save the World

On the last perfect day beside the last perfect body
of water, we get infected with a persistently bad idea.
We cancel our appointment with a squalling therapist.
You are smiling, you are emptying the world
so we can be alone. But who would dare to exist,
just for that? It's spring, bitch, be in love.
When you were in a ditch, I was in a ditch.
They were different ditches, but there we were
waiting for one another like a phantom limb.
I've made the stupidly courageous act
of letting our loudmouthed scars fall in love.
The daisies beside us are closing their mouths
in anticipation of what comes next.
I recognize this is the actual end
because I finally feel alive.
I'm hawk-eyeing your hairline
as you talk about your youth in Florida.
Were you there then, too, looking out from the pier
wondering if there could be someone out there
just as strange as you?
The waves have started to crest
as you speak French; the dogs cease
their yawps. I still my mind to ride your tongue.
I am terrified of wide-open spaces,
all the possibilities of someone with ill intentions.
I'm fighting my thoughts of Florida again,
the nightclub, the forty-nine phones scuffing the floor
like downed birds. I was not there,
but I will never be the same.
Tell me again (in French) the word for pulse.
Let us rename what we have to remember.
I don't think I will ever not be afraid again.

Off Camera There Is a Beach & a Party

And to tell the truth I don't want to let go of the wrists
of idleness, I don't want to sell my life for money,
I don't even want to come in out of the rain.

—MARY OLIVER

Cage

1a: A box or place of confinement for birds and other animals (or, in barbarous times, for human beings), made wholly or partly of wire, or with bars of metal or wood, so as to admit air and light, while preventing the creature's escape

2a: A prison for petty malefactors

4b: A scaffold, elevated stage, or seat

5b: The barrel of a whim on which the rope is wound; a drum

I am always sitting facing the exit, I am always in the back row, I am always waiting for you to somehow, monstrously and impossibly, enter the shot.

Soundtrack

"I Can't Stand the Rain" by Ann Peebles

Ritual

On the possibility that there are still birds
where you are, leave debris in the limbs for their nest
    stockpile.
Think: loose underwear elastic, an abuser's shredded
    transcript, Easter cellophane grass.
Always carry a Ziploc.
Name every bird who takes something from your
    offering after a name you can't make yourself say.
Call to them all the time with your little handfuls of
    waste and your grandmother's Depression-era
    hoarding tendency keepsies.
Coo, motherfucker, who cares what the neighbors say.

Does He Like You or Is He Just Midwestern?

We are sitting in the front yard
and I, too, want the end of something.

A prairie, a dark house, an empty car
running in the cult of midwinter death.

I say, *Your body told me*
in a dream it wasn't afraid of anything.

If I were to be completely honest,
I don't think either of us could handle what I want:

give me boundless love and handfuls of Valium.
You sort of bring the desert with you.

I am radiant in the bombglow echoing
across the county line. We should fuck wherever we want.

Honey, suckle from my furried tit since there's a bad moon
rising and I hear hurricanes blowing.

I have loved you all my life;
all my life I have loved you.

Between the curtains of bombs, I wait
for you smoking at the cornfield stage door.

The Only Living Boys in New York

It was the year of gas masks & no more
coffee or grocery-store trips.

We've gone about this new kind of living
nonchalantly—our bed, five hundred cans of food.

I will know you have made it
back by raising the mailbox bannered arm.

At night, in bed beside me, we describe magnolias
and what scent comes with an acidless breeze.

Our mornings are mostly spent looking out
the window at what dogs are left

dragging the liquor man's family down
the street where a whole horde of Tim Johnsons

rip them belly to limb to bone.
The day the bomb dropped on this island

that you loved, some simply jumped
out shutterless windows or off buildings. Who wants

to feel the death-cloud cover them like a wave?
We agreed that a watermelon splitting

was the closest sound for all the Fallers—that if
either you or I should not come

back, the other would not go looking.
Stay in the house with the world's last songbird.

Bathing together, we count each other's cuts
while he chirps & chirps & chirps.

One day, either you or I will walk out
onto the courtyard—thinking it months ago—maskless

and it will feel like the sea came in;
it will be an eternal September.

You'll think you smell honeysuckle;
you'll think my arm is around you;

You'll hear the bluest of blues far off singing.
Which do you miss most—

the body or the shadow?

The Devil Rules This World Because He Created It and That God Is Far Away

You would think we'd be ashamed
for outliving our friends and fellow Americans.
We're not. Our nationalist faith is so strong
it makes everyone uncomfortable.
A hummingbird is sobbing during office hours;
they're coming to take the hummingbird's family.
It is a felony to house a hummingbird.
Who even reports a hummingbird?
Clearly, I mean a human when I say a hummingbird.
It is a sin to make a bird a metaphor for a person.
The young woman is sobbing during office hours;
they're coming to take the young woman's family.
It is a felony to house the young woman.
Who even reports a young woman?
Clearly, I mean a human when I say a human.

The Devil Has Been Busy Today

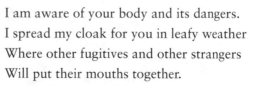

I am aware of your body and its dangers.
I spread my cloak for you in leafy weather
Where other fugitives and other strangers
Will put their mouths together.

—THOMAS JAMES

Rape

1a: Unlawful sexual activity and usually sexual intercourse carried out forcibly or under threat of injury against a person's will or with a person who is beneath a certain age or incapable of valid consent because of mental illness, mental deficiency, intoxication, unconsciousness, or deception

2a: An outrageous violation

3a: An act or instance of robbing or despoiling or carrying away a person by force

4: The pomace of grapes left after expression of the juice

See Apocalypse.

Soundtrack

"Gimme Shelter" by Merry Clayton

Ritual

Make breakfast for supper.

Pleasure yourself every chance you get.

Orgasm to a game show.

Put on a live recording of a broken-up band or a
    dead solo act. Stop cleaning and clap along
    with the applause.

Learn to say "thank you" and "I'm sorry" in at
    least three living languages and two dead ones.

Light a stick of Nag champa and write a politician
    to go get fucked.

Release Your Fear: The War Cries of Hummingbirds

Your car radio is the kind of broken
in which it'll only play ELO
because it's a stuck cassette
and the tips need to go toward heat.
The breakup happens near the freeway
in between the left turn signal's beep.
The magic is the fucking song finally changing,
the moment of surreal explosion, a Ferris wheel in reverse.
I just want you in my head,
my little, dirty mongrel mind,
listening until the loop takes over
its own mad orchestra.

You wanted the end to have been fireworks in February,
you wanted it to be all watercolor runoff.
The tornado named Samantha comes into the bar and kisses you
and slams her purse of broken men beside me.
She drinks all the freebies and bats her eyes at you at me.
The blue Earth turns black when she says *so, who are you again?*
And you fill her up, pour us a round, and try to give me some light.
When you two walk out, you leave me with my hips: a hungry tidal wave.
This is another wreck, another reason to let the birds play with my hair again.

You drink until
the face behind you is your favorite dead blond boy.
You count their money like communion,
genuflect like the rug's quicksand.
Name your next brokenhearted storm after me.
Count the floating men
as I close their eyes,
take my lips to their neck-nape
and say *Try again, try again you goddamn little fool.*

This Must Be the Place

My rapist's driving
to work and the traffic is terrible.

My rapist's wife
is driving and cackling at a podcast.

My rapist's high school
friend just had a baby, mazel.

My rapist's old neighbor
lost her foot in a car wreck.

My rapist's coworker
laughed at one of his rape jokes, again.

My rapist's accountant
is getting suspicious of the hush.

My rapist's mailman
gets candy on Christmas like his grandma did.

My rapist's checkout person
hates his smugness.

My rapist's hometown
cancels school to harvest Virginia tobacco.

My rapist's church
was my church.

My rapist's friends
are my friends.

My rapist's mother
is my mother's sister.

My rapist's reading
this poem and looking for his name.

My rapist's name
starts with a B.

You Knew
There Had to
Be a Reckoning

It is impossible to move
in all that white.
　　　　—Thomas James

Statute Of Limitations

1a: A statute assigning a certain time after which rights cannot be enforced by legal action or offenses cannot be punished

In 2020, Virginia House Bill 610 was introduced by Jason S. Miyares, R-82nd, of Virginia Beach. This bill creates a two-year time period, from after July 1, 2020, but before July 1, 2022, in which persons can file a claim for injury from sexual abuse occurring before the age of 18, regardless of whether the statute of limitations expired.

Soundtrack

"I Shall Be Released" by Mama Cass, Mary Travers, and Joni Mitchell

Ritual

In a public space,
make yourself openly weep
with whatever media assistance you
    may need:
Bambi, *Brokeback Mountain*,
    revisionist American history,
the military and the prison industrial
    complexes.
If you are unable to cry,
see a therapist already.
Smoke 'em if you got 'em.

Gay $

How can I not reach where you are

And pull you back. How can I be
And you not. You're forever on the platform
——MARY JO BANG

Research shows that the songbird
dreams of singing, I dream
of you, sick, finding you
like a recovered rusty lockbox.

This world was not made
with our dancing in mind,
but you did like along a fissure.
What I want: a multiverse
where: you still clank
vodkas over Pall Malls,
where: you are safe
in rain-lashed gardens
of marigolds and misfits,
where: you're on the brink of green
and young and pretty.

They treated you in this world
like an impossible receptionist.
They treated you like someone
else's mess to mop up.
They touched you like a used
Kleenex left on a public surface.
As you lay dying, the women held you
like a telephone, like on a honeymoon.
Making love like tangled roller-coasters
didn't kill you, capitalism did.

While all the men were dying,
Chicago stood around strangely
like a horse (in your bedroom)
making things cry.
They drove by just to see if lights're on.
When a body cannot consume,
it cannot contribute to America.
There is intentionality behind
everything, especially the silence
of neighbors, coworkers, empty streets,
the erasure of you from the city.
Did you ever imagine me then
like I imagine you now: gay $,
gay apartment, gay hair
beautiful like a coiffed cruise liner?
The great resistance will start
with remembering, the need not
for another world, but this one
made if only a little bearable for you to sing.

Fetch the Bolt Cutters

Seven kids and dead at twenty-three, Benjamin Franklin
Russell Price, you started some mess.
I only found you because I was lonely
and had nowhere to go
and no money to do anything with.
The dark woods have been replaced
with the dark web. Having fun isn't hard
when you've got a library card. You probably had one book
and we know what that was. What is in us
that makes us start back south
and end up in a flyover state?
We always saddleback in Virginia.
Next door, they discovered
Mountain Dew and every October since
we've walked Main Street sweet breath
hands begging for some Pepsi-Cola-signed relief.
Yesterday in a city that wasn't here
when you were in an A-line maxi skirt
Mary Sturgill would have loved and been hung for
I thought about all the evil in our family.
I've been trying to measure my pain
against y'all's. John James had sixteen kids
in twenty years. We never all seem to make it.
You, Benjamin Franklin Russell Price,
were dead at twenty-three, but nowhere says what of.
Now our people can read and write,
but they don't. Our family has always lived
with something scratching in the walls.
I'm writing about you in the heat
of another preventable disaster.
A friend who comes to me through a trauma machine
used a website and found an entire family she never knew of.
Maybe I'm wanting some tragic secret to be resolved,
maybe I'm just tired of our poverty line.

Get this shit, I saw your census, the taker's cursive
CA on "Survivor of the Confederate or Union Army."
I hope you're fucking burning in hell, traitor.
At our community's last reenactment of the North's invasion of our
     homeland,
this dumbshit punk kid next to me asked his dumbshit mom if the South wins
this year. I should practice empathy, but I'm tired of our Southernness
always being both a caricature and a blistering truth.
We've probably always been acceptable white trash wherever we've been.
I guess you'd be proud of some parts of this family,
I hope I'm pissing you off. I spend all day trying to get y'all
to see how we got where we are. All the bastards in this family
will get their due. Maybe I'm wrong about Mary loving this dress,
maybe I'm wrong about assuming your transphobia. Maybe everything isn't
     completely fucked.
In an imagined seance, all y'all look up at me from below and regret your
     transactions
and acknowledge that you were too poor to enslave people during your time
and beg for my forgiveness for your complacency and say you love my eye
     makeup
and you weep enough Confederate-funded salt to warrant a historical marker
and when I look down to you, with my amazing eye makeup, I say, *After all
     this time,*
you'll be tickled shitless to know that one good ol' boy still loves the CSA.
More members of our clan will be joining you momentarily.
I say to my dead fuckhead relatives across time and space:
I am the product of your nightmares, all suffering is suffering,
we can have green thumbs and problematic politics.
We know hunger like a sibling.
Everyone around us is always dying it seems. That we can agree on.
When my grandmother was dying, I lied and said I had finished a happy
     book on the apocalypse.
I had my mama show her, deathbed-ridden, my chapbook TONIGHT WE
     FUCK THE TRAILER PARK OUT OF EACH OTHER in capital letters across
     the cover, and my mama said it was called A HAPPY BOOK ON THE
     APOCALYPSE.

Nanny was blind with pain meds and said *how pretty what a nice cover*
   Russell would be proud.
Even if you think you died with a secret, it takes two to keep it.
Did they fucking rhyme in your time?
One dude on our tree lived to be ninety-one. Why, though?
With a name like Hezekial, he had to be queer and beautiful.
How far we are from all of you and still we're tilling stolen land with bad
   teeth and weak hearts.
The night I made myself a bridegroom to the doomsday I took my dead
   grandfather's name,
all the rotted limbs branch out like an acceptable eyesore. I'm taking
   everything back.
I think it's safe to assume two things: 1) y'all would love Fiona Apple and
   Amy Winehouse, too, & 2) the family line dies with me.

It's a Nice Day to Start Again, It's a Nice Day for a White Wedding

I see you
near the snail-peddling sea
hoarding pinches
of sand
wasting time with
birds
     —PABLO NERUDA

Naming

1a: To give (a person or thing) a specified name

1b: With distinguishing word: to have a (good or bad) reputation

1d: To be said to be

2a: A descriptive, often disparaging, epithet

3b: To call by the right name; to recognize or identify correctly

6b: To utter, say (a word). *Obsolete.*

*Their names are B— H———— and B— M————
and they know what they did.*

Soundtrack

"This Is the Day" by The The

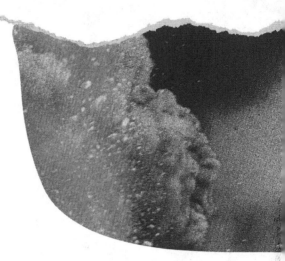

Ritual

Borrow a blue light bulb
from someone who looks
like they probably have one.

Read this aloud,
naked, and alone in the glow.
How close is midnight on the Doomsday Clock?
What color is the magic you've been working so far?
Buy a low-maintenance houseplant and think
    yourself a forgiving and caring god.
Tell someone you love them;
tomorrow, take it back.

Apocalypse with Eyeliner

I believe in past lives.
I wasn't dead, just waiting
around for you.
A corner in Rogers Park,
in line at Target,
the stranger at a birthday party . . .
According to your ascending sign
and the twenty-buck psychic,
you were born to bury me.
My body: a shoebox of histories
it never wanted.
The night you beat me
I became a highway-
lined wildflower field.
When the plane covers me
in an insecticide cloud,
I turn into toxic honeysuckle.
You let your future
children feed
on me. Their tongues
swell and they chant, chant, chant
my name back to you.

Notes

"Human Flesh Search Engine" (*renrou sousuo yinqing*) is a Chinese term describing online information sharing in a collective effort to learn forbidden or taboo material, often geared toward vigilante exposure of social and criminal offenses.

"There Will Come Soft Rains and the Smell of the Ground" is the first line of Sara Teasdale's poem "There Will Come Soft Rains" (1918). The full poem reads:

(War Time)

There will come soft rains and the smell of the ground,
And swallows circling with their shimmering sound;

And frogs in the pools singing at night,
And wild plum trees in tremulous white,

Robins will wear their feathery fire
Whistling their whims on a low fence-wire;

And not one will know of the war, not one
Will care at last when it is done.

Not one would mind, neither bird nor tree
If mankind perished utterly;

And Spring herself, when she woke at dawn,
Would scarcely know that we were gone.

In the poem "Armageddon Origin Story," the line "Flood's not the answer, people just float" is from Tony Kushner's play *Angels in America*.

In "Mr. Doomsday," the phrase "I'm getting that T-shirt wet" was overheard in a gang altercation on my street in 2014. A teenage boy was instigated by a superior to "Wet that T-shirt up!" upon seeing a rival gang member on the street. Both teenage boys survived the shooting, but a man who just happened to be waiting for the bus at that time did not.

"But about That Day or Hour No One Knows, Not Even the Angels . . ." comes from Matthew 24:36 and Matthew 24:40.

The title "Someone Is Missing for You and the Whole World Feels Empty" is a riff on the Joan Didion line "A single person is missing for you, and the whole world is empty." The favorite song is "In-A-Gadda-Da-Vida" by Iron Butterfly. The nickname "Coyote" is also a reference to the Joni Mitchell song.

In the poem "If You Want Space, Join NASA," the line "sing into your mouth" is from "This Must Be the Place" by the Talking Heads.

The "seven trumpets" in "On When They Say Hustling . . ." is a reference to the apocalyptic visions of John of Patmos in the book of Revelation.

"I Did an Ugly Thing Once, but It Was in a Beautiful Room" gets its title from *Tonight, I'm Someone Else: Essays* by Chelsea Hodson. Language in this poem was inspired, lifted, siphoned from: *Clay: Poems* by David Groff, the Strokes, Frank O'Hara, misheard Fleetwood Mac, the Divinyls.

"The Tsunami Was Not a Metaphor. For a Full Day I Was the Drowning Wave" is a line by Chicago writer Marty McConnell.

"Then, Brother, Get Back, 'Cause My Breast's Gonna Bust Open" takes its title from the song "Every Single Night" by Fiona Apple. "We were never about butterflies" is a line by the Russian poet Anna Akhmatova.

"My Sweetheart Is a Drunkard, Lord . . ." is a cento of lines by Thomas James from his collection *Letters to a Stranger*. James was a queer Illinoisian writer who died by the act of suicide shortly after the publication of his first book in 1973.

"I Heard Somebody Say, 'Disco Inferno, Burn This Mother Down'" is a lyric from "Disco Inferno" by the Trammps.

"I Think We're Alone Now: Your Lips, My Lips, Apocalypse" is a mashup of two song lyrics, one by Tiffany and the other by Cigarettes After Sex.

"Dance Yourself Clean" is after the song of the same title by LCD Soundsytem.

The poem "How to Stay Politically Active While Fucking the Existential Dread Away" lifts language or alludes to the following artists: Peaches, Lana Del Rey, Birdie, Miike Snow, the Spice Girls, Crosby, Stills, and Nash, Jewel, Joanna Newsom, Frank O'Hara, and Mandy Moore. The Closet opened as a lesbian bar in Chicago in 1978.

In the poem "When Someone Asks My Gender, I Say a Nonexistent Month," the lines "I'm going to be a lady one day; I don't know when or how" are from the song "Fancy," written and recorded by Bobbie Gentry in 1969 and later covered by Reba McEntire.

The subtitle of "Ars Poetica: We Can Take Our Turn, Singing Them Dirty Rap Songs" is a lyric from "Crazy Rap (Colt 45)" by Afroman. "Give me all that you can't pick up the phone and tell someone" is based on Frank O'Hara's manifesto on Personism. "I've got something for his punk ass" is a lyric from "Santeria" by Sublime. "Write it" quotes Elizabeth Bishop's "One Art." "Yoshimi" is from "Yoshimi Battles the Pink Robots" by the Flaming Lips.

In the poem "My Sexual Identity Is a Toaster in a Bathtub," the lines "I'm the kind of guy who laughs at a funeral— / can't understand what I mean, you soon will . . ." are from the song "One Week" by Barenaked Ladies.

"Mr. Blue Sky" is a reference to the song of the same name by Electric Light Orchestra. "I've got so much honey, the bees envy me" is from "My Girl" by the Temptations and is intended to be sung aloud, on key and on beat, at the end of this poem.

"Trying to Catch a Deluge in a Paper Cup" is a lyric from "Don't Dream It's Over" by Crowded House.

The poem "It Passed for Feathers" is a cento using language borrowed from Robyn Schiff's book *Worth* (University of Iowa Press, 2002).

"Now Comes in the Fuckery" is a line from the podcast *The Read*.

In the poem "A Love Poem Will Not Save the World," the line "just as strange as you" is a reference to the Frida Kahlo quote, "I used to think I was the strangest person in the world but then I thought there are so many people in the world, there must be someone just like me who feels bizarre and flawed in the same ways I do. I would imagine her, and imagine that she must be out there thinking of me, too. Well, I hope that if you are out there and read this and know that, yes, it's true I'm here, and I'm just as strange as you." The poem commemorates the mass shooting at Pulse, a gay nightclub in Orlando, Florida, in June 2016.

"Does He Like You or Is He Just Midwestern" takes its title from an article published on the feminist satire website *Reductress*. "Bad moon rising and I hear hurricanes blowing" comes from the song "Bad Moon Rising" by Creedence Clearwater Revival.

"The Only Living Boys in New York" is a reference to the Simon and Garfunkel song "The Only Living Boy in New York." Tim Johnson is the name of the rabid dog in *To Kill a Mockingbird* by Harper Lee.

"Gay $" is a reference to the direct action initiative spearheaded by Chicagoan Marge Summit. In response to the AIDS epidemic, gay bars stamped the phrase "Gay $" on paper money to demonstrate gay economic power, to increase visibility of the illness, and to protest the lack of social engagement in response.

"Fetch the Bolt Cutters" takes its title from the song and album of the same name by Fiona Apple. The title comes from a line spoken by Gillian Anderson in the British-Irish show *The Fall*. Upon discovering where a young woman is being tortured and held captive, Anderson puts on rubber gloves and commands her fellow officer to "fetch the bolt cutters."

"It's a Nice Day to Start Again, It's a Nice Day for a White Wedding" is a lyric from the song "White Wedding" by Billy Idol. In the "naming" section, I intended to name the abusive men in my family, but the publisher prohibited it for legal reasons. One was a rapist and the other was a kid-beater. Over the six years it has taken to write this book, forty-some people have read the name of my rapist, and prior to this book's publication, the extended statute of limitations had not expired, giving me time to call the Washington County, Virginia, sheriff's office at any minute and say, *Hey, it's me again. I have a name.* In a cloud, I've saved his confession.

Acknowledgments

I'm grateful to the following journals in which some of these poems first appeared: the *Adroit Journal*, *Anarchist Review of Books*, *Boston Review*, *Court Green*, *DIAGRAM*, *Dream Pop Press*, *EOAGH*, *Glitterwolf*, *Guesthouse*, *The HIV Here & Now Project*, *Iron Horse Literary Review*, *Jet Fuel Review*, *Lambda Literary*, *Nimrod International Journal of Prose and Poetry*, *Motionpoems*, *PANK*, and *Voicemail Poems*.

The following organizations supported the creation of this book and I am forever grateful: 3Arts Illinois, the American Writers Museum, the Claire Rosen and Samuel Edes Foundation, Illinois Humanities, the Illinois Arts Council, the Guild Literary Complex, the Lambda Foundation, Northwestern University, Patrick Henry High School (of Glade Spring, Virginia), PEN America, the Poetry Brothel, the Poetry Center of Chicago, the Poetry Foundation, the Ragdale Foundation, Sibling Rivalry Press, the University of Virginia, and Women & Children First Bookstore (in Chicago).

For my family (blood and found) who guided me through all the stages of this book, who let me get a little dirty with dynamite and love me anyway. Mom, Dad, Ashley, Felicity, and Walker. Special thanks to my coven: Bryan Borland, Kayleb Rae Candrilli, Hannah Gamble, Joe Osmundson, Justin Paxton, Maggie Smith, Peter Solowy, Tara Stringfellow, my therapist SugarRae, Kelly Sundberg, Ian Vogt, Nick White, and Paul Wildfeuer. If I want to thank you, I'll do it in person; and if I want to no thank you, I'll do that in person, too.

This book would not exist were it not for the guidance and unwavering support of Parneshia Jones and her entire rockstar lineup of a team (especially the Annes and JD) at Northwestern University Press. We all learned a lot about each other in this process. Up the punk.

This book was written on stolen land previously inhabited by people of the following Native nations: Bodéwadmiakiwen (Potawatomi), Cherokee, Hoocąk (Ho-Chunk), Kiikaapoi (Kickapoo), Myaamia, Očhéthi Šakówiŋ, Peoria, and Yuchi.

A portion of the royalties earned from the sale of this book will be donated to the Glade Spring public library, SWOPS (Sex Workers Outreach Project of Chicago), The Trevor Project, and RAINN (Rape, Abuse, Incest National Network). There was a time when you helped me; it's my turn now.